An Introduction to

Forex Trading
Using Price Action

MICHELLE MICHAELS

DISCLAIMER

This book is designed to provide information that the author believes to be accurate on the subject matter it covers, but it is sold with the understanding that neither the author nor the publisher is offering individualized advice tailored to any specific portfolio or to any individual's particular needs, or rendering investment advice or other professional services such as legal accounting advice. Professional services should be sought if one needs expert assistance in areas that include investment, legal, and accounting advice.

There is a substantial risk of loss associated with trading these markets. Losses can and will occur. No system or methodology has ever been developed that can guarantee profits or ensure freedom from losses. No representation or implication is being made that using this information will generate profits or ensure freedom from losses. The trade examples provided were hypothetical only and were prepared with the benefit of hindsight. No hypothetical trading record can completely account for the impact of financial risk in actual live trading. Additionally, this book is not intended to serve as the basis for any financial decisions, as a recommendation of a specific trading system. Your personal financial circumstances must be considered carefully before investing or spending money.

No warranty is made with respect to the accuracy or completeness of the information contained herein, and both the author and the publisher specifically disclaim any responsibility for any liability, loss or risk, personal or otherwise, which is incurred as a consequence, directly or indirectly, of the use and application of any of the contents of this book.

CONTENTS

1

WHAT IS PRICE ACTION TRADING?

Price Action trading is the study of the price movement of the market, which enables the trader to identify the next possible market move. There is a saying in the forex market; *"History repeats itself"*. The successful Price Action trader has the capacity to make smart decisions taking a trade with the proper knowledge of how to study the raw price data to master the "Price Action". There are thousands of strategies and rules for making a profit from the Forex market, so why do some traders trade the Forex market with the Price Action strategy? The simple answer is that this form of trading provides a high percentage of winning trades, along with a clear and logical explanation for each trade.

Three major benefits of Price Action Trading

1. Raw price movement helps to get a clear insight of the current market conditions.
2. Price Action trading helps you to make a logical decision with excellent risk-reward ratio.
3. Helps you to develop a simple and effective trading system for becoming a successful trader.

Is this the type of trading style that might suit you? If so, then let's get into it.

There are some important tools that successful traders and professional fund managers use while they trade with raw price data. Professional fund managers, you may ask? Yes, you read correctly! Professional traders and fund managers who trade the raw price can make consistent profits year in year out.

Important technical tools for Price Action Trading

- Support and Resistance Levels.
- Trend lines and Channels.
- Chart Patterns.
- Swing High and Swing Low Levels.

Rising popularity of Price Action Trading

There are so many different strategies which claim to be extremely profitable. However, the simplicity and clarity of Price Action trading is astounding compared to other trading methodologies. High probability trades are easily filtered out through proper technical and fundamental analysis in the Price Action trading Setup. But success will not necessarily come easy. Most successful traders have experienced a difficult past as well as frustration trading in the real life market. But eventually over time, they develop self-discipline and master the art of trading using Price Action only.

2

CANDLESTICK PATTERNS

There are three major charts widely used in Forex trading:

1. Line Chart
2. Bar Chart
3. Candlestick Chart

Many consider the candlestick chart to be the most important of charts when it comes to Price Action trading. What is a candlestick? A candlestick represents the price movement of a currency pair for a definite interval of time. For instance, a candlestick formed on a 1-hour chart represents the last 1-hour of price action.

Facts behind the trending popularity of Candlesticks

It's the number one tool that the Price Action traders use for analyzing the market sentiment as it helps to identify:

- Volatility
- Session high and low
- Opening and closing price
- High profitable trading signals
- Risk reward ratio

Before we go further into price action trading, let's go through some important candlestick patterns along with their interpretation. Price Action traders make their trade decisions based on highly reliable candlestick patterns formed in or around significant areas of the Forex Market. So what are significant areas? The Forex market tends to respect certain areas for a long period of time, and these are known as support and resistance levels. The support and resistance levels are commonly termed as significant areas.

Let's start our lesson.

How do we read a candlestick?

A simple example will help you to understand this better.

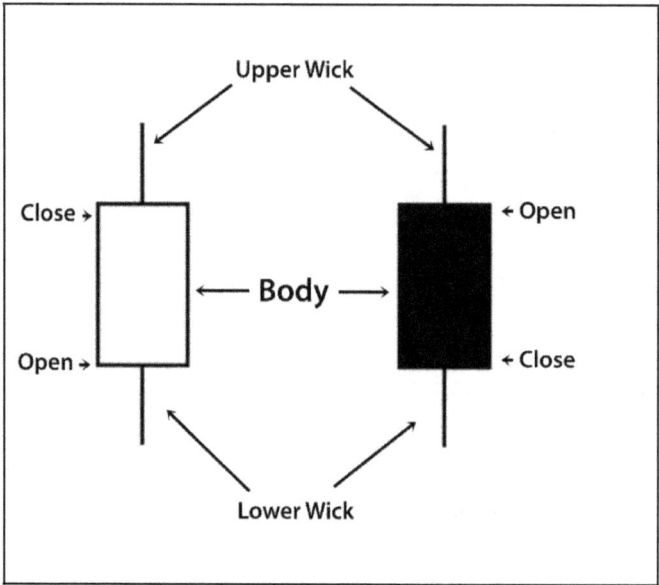

The body shows the relative movement of price from its opening to closing time. The upper wick *(often referred to as a shadow)* indicates the highest price and lower wick (shadow) indicates the lowest price for definite time period. It is as simple as that.

As a Price Action trader, you must know the 15 important candlesticks and their relative meaning. Confused? Don't worry; the following will make it a lot easier to understand.

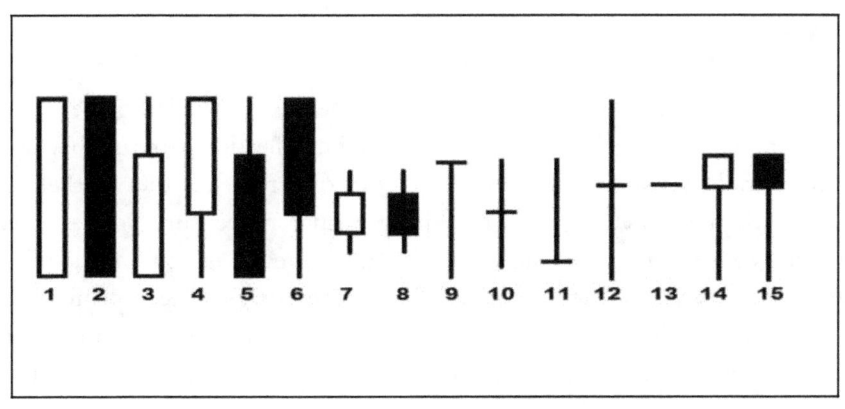

Candlestick	Name	Signal
1	Big white body or white Marubozu	Very Bullish
2	Big black body or black Marubozu	Very Bearish
3	White opening Marubozu	Quite Bullish
4	White closing Marubozu	Bullish
5	Black closing Marubozu	Bearish
6	Black opening Marubozu	Quite Bearish
7	White Candle	No direction
8	Black Candle	No direction
9	Dragon Fly Doji	Potential reversal
10	Doji Star	Potential reversal
11	Gravestone Doji	Stable/Reversal
12	Long Legged Doji	Reversal
13	Four Price Doji	Reversal
14	Hammer (White)	Top/Bottom reversal
15	Hammer (Black)	Top/Bottom reversal

Once you have memorized this candlestick chart, then you are one step closer to becoming a Price Action trader! Simply by determining the chart and candlestick, you will be able to make a logical decision whether to buy or sell. Hold on a minute though!

A group of candlesticks together forms a stable pattern which gives a very reliable signal in the forex market. Before going into the next Section, you should familiarize yourself with the candlestick chart again.

Candle Stick Patterns

Most successful Forex traders like the confluence of signals before getting into a trade. These are some of the preferred candlestick patterns that Price Action traders use in order to find the direction of the market. As mentioned a moment ago, before progressing, make sure you are very familiar with the previous single candlestick patterns as you will definitely need to know them back to front, if you want to become a professional Price Action trader. These candlestick patterns are simply the combination of one or more single candlesticks that you learned in the previous chart.

The top 5 most reliable candlestick patterns

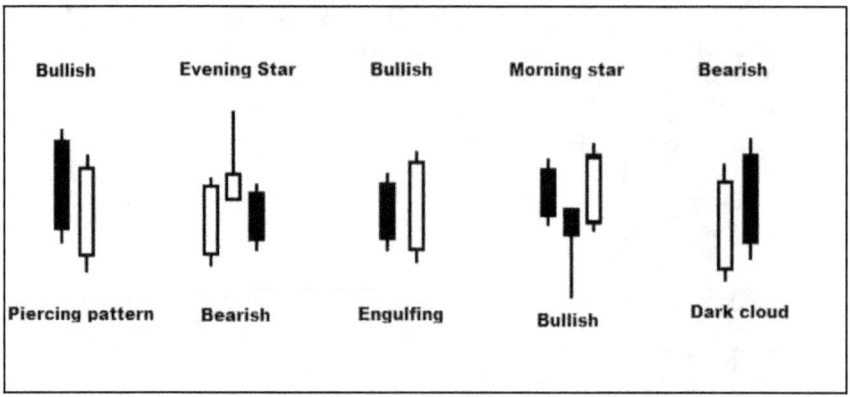

Sounds pretty simple doesn't it? So, how do we trade with these candlestick patterns? Bear with me, as this information will be provided in the next Section.

3

IMPORTANT TIME FRAMES FOR PRICE ACTION TRADERS

Every successful trader has their own working strategies. Strategies are not developed in a day, rather they are the result of perseverance and dedicated practice. Choosing a time frame is paramount for the trader since it's the key ingredient for keeping to a stable trading strategy. So, which time is best for trading? There are no hard and fast answers to this question. The time frame is chosen based on the trader's personality and trading style. A 5-minute chart displays all the required information a scalper would require, but for a Swing or Position trader, a longer time frame would be more suitable.

Choosing the right time frame in the beginning can be very frustrating. Many new traders incur heavy losses due to the improper selection of a time frame. Without prioritizing specific time frames, traders can also get confused. For instance, a 5-minute chart is giving a clear buy signal and on the contrary, the 30-minute chart has the best sell signal you have ever seen. How do you deal with this situation? Well, the way to deal with this is to use multiple time frame analysis which will be discussed in Section 4 of this book.

Selecting the best time frame

Before selecting your preferred time frame let's have a quick look at these questions.

- Are you Scalper?
- Do you prefer day trading?
- Are you a swing or position trader?

Trading time frames will greatly depend on the trading style of a trader. A scalper generally trades in shorter time frames with high frequency. Their main objective is to make a profit from the quick and small movements of the market. So, what time frame do they use? If you are thinking shorter time frame, then you are absolutely right. They would be looking at tick, 1-min, 2- min, 3-min, 5-min, 10-min and possibly 15-min charts.

Day traders and swing traders prefer the longer time frames. They generally keep their trades open longer than a scalper, which can be anything from several minutes to several days. Keep in mind that trading the higher time frames generally creates a better result due to higher quality signals and the removal of a lot of the market noise.

The professional traders don't trade with the use of a single time frame, rather they make the best logical decision through multiple time frame analysis. This will be covered in the next Section where, you will master how to do multiple time frame analysis.

4

MULTIPLE TIME FRAME ANALYSIS

Trading the forex market is very easy when you know how! A successful trader can correctly identify a trade and potential reversal point. So how do they do it? A number of factors are behind their success. Multiple time frame analysis is one of the most important factors.

Preferred time frames used by different traders

- Scalpers: Prefer shorter time frame charts.

- Day traders: Prefer medium time frame charts.

- Position or swing traders: Prefer longer time frame charts.

What is multiple time frame analysis?

Making logical decisions from two or more different time frame charts is commonly known as multiple time frame analysis. The longer time frame is generally used to identify the trades whereas the shorter time frame helps us to get into a trade. So basically the longer time frame will assist with choosing the correct trade direction (preferred trend) and the shorter time frame will assist the trader make a more specific entry into that trend.

Let's look at an example on the following page.

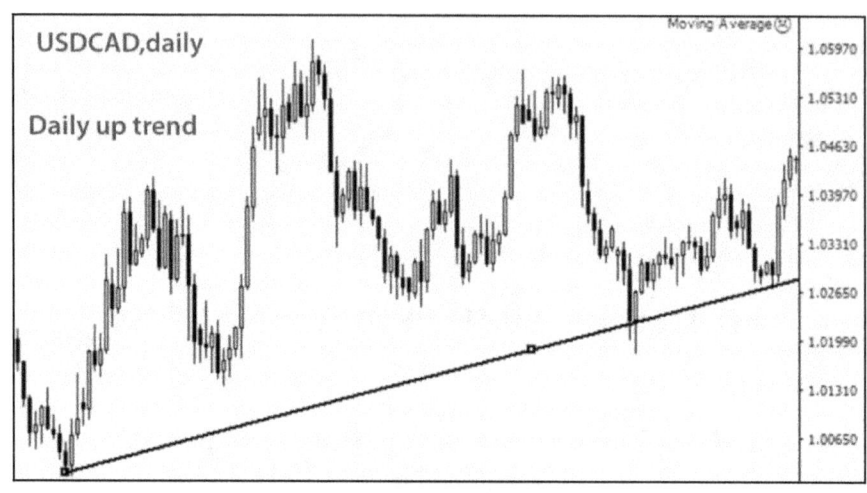

Figure: Trader using the daily chart to identify the "Bullish Trend"

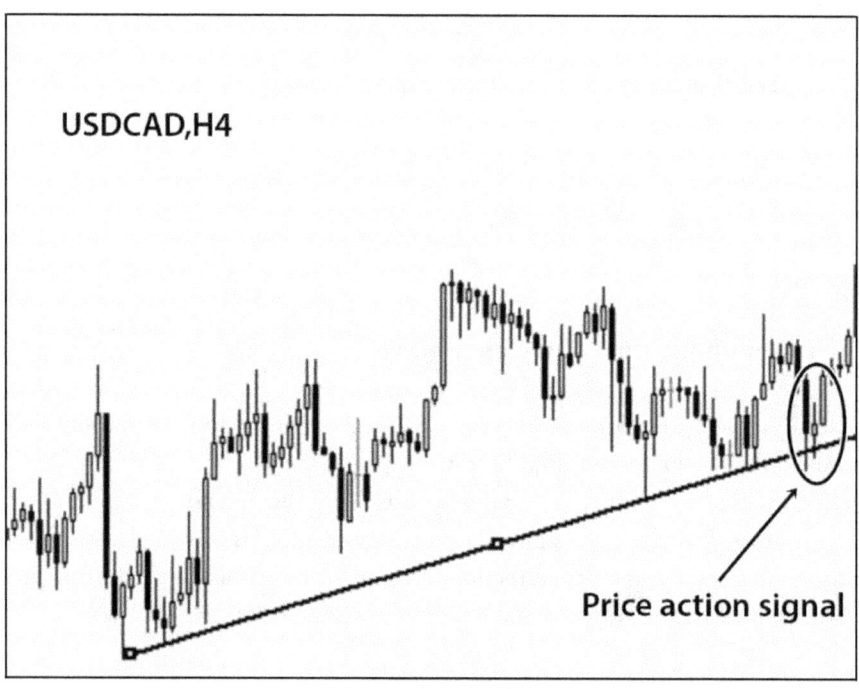

Figure: "Price Action" confirmation in 4 hour chart

Detailed explanation

First of all, successful traders use a higher time frame to identify the prevailing trend in the market. In the above figure the trader spots a valid uptrend in USD/CAD with the help of a trend line. The market is making successive *"Higher High"* which is a good sign of a bullish trend.

Once the trader identifies the prevailing trend in the market, he or she would then go to the next step - Trade execution! The smaller time frame allows the trader to take a more precise entry. On the 4 hour chart, a strong uptrend is also noticed with a price action signal (Morning Star) on the trend line. This unique combination of taking a trade through multiple time frame analysis can give a higher percentage of winning trades.

5

HOW TO DRAW PERFECT SUPPORT AND RESISTANCE LEVELS

It may sound surprising but support and resistance are the most important parameters in Forex Trading regardless of trading style and strategy. These levels give us the potential entry point to enter into a trade. As a Price Action trader you must know how to draw perfect support and resistance (S/R) levels. These are the potential two areas which tell us the market's next move.

Three possible scenarios of price action in S/R levels:

- A minor or major retrace in the trend

- Change of prevailing trend

- Ranging market

Support and resistance area of a currency pair

Yes, you have read correctly! Support and resistance levels are much better when we see it as an area instead of an exact level. When considering an area as a support or resistance zone, we must find rejection of price at least on two occasions. I will give you three simple rules for drawing perfect support and resistance zones.

Three cardinal rules for drawing support and resistance zones

1. Price must reject a certain area or zone at least twice.

2. A Higher number of rejections results in a stronger support and resistance area.

3. Recent swing highs, swing lows and rejections are preferred.

Facts about support and resistance levels

Basically, the support area helps the market to climb up while the resistance area restricts the upward momentum of a market. Imagine support being like a floor below you and resistance being the ceiling above you. Significant support and resistance levels are not broken easily. Strong economic news releases or other high impact economic activities are required in order to overcome these significant levels or zones. Traders usually try to find a buying opportunity at a support zone and look for a selling opportunity at a resistance zone.

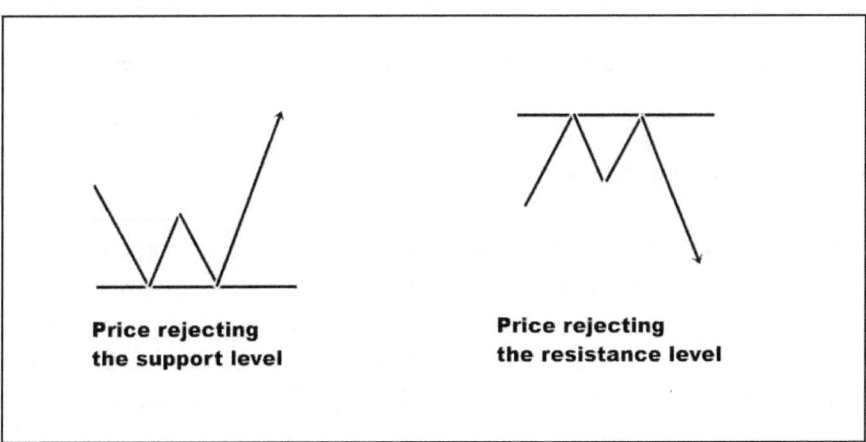

Price rejecting the support level

Price rejecting the resistance level

That's it! Let's start buying at the support and selling the at resistance levels. Hold on! These levels are not going to hold the market forever. Sometimes they will be broken and cause the prevailing trend to change. That's why some professional traders use the Price Action trading strategy to determine the validity of support and resistance levels.

Let's look at an example of how a professional trader rides 900+ pips in the GBP/USD.

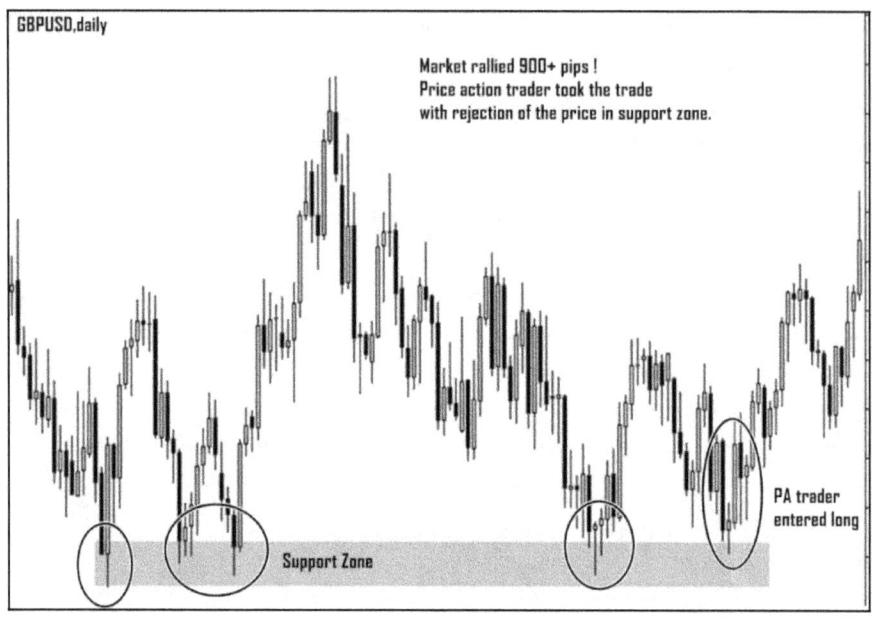

Figure: Taking long in significant support area along with price action confirmation

Perfect Price Action setup

The above trade is a classic example of a perfectly drawn support zone. *"Note that many traders call this support zone as support area."* The price rejected the important support area twice. Successful traders will wait patiently for their perfect timing. Guess what! The market retraced back into the support area for the third time and forms a reliable rejection pattern known as "Pin Bar". After the "Pin Bar," a series of doji followed by a big white candle confirms the trade signal. Can you remember the big white candle? If not then go back to Section 2 for a quick review. Are you becoming a fan of price action trading yet? There will be some more interesting stuff coming up next.

6

PRICE ACTION TRADING SETUP AT SUPPORT AND RESISTANCE LEVELS

In the previous Section, we learnt how to draw perfect support and resistance levels or zones. You have also seen a classic example of price action trading using a support zone. Now it is time to get into a little more detail. So when do we start? We have already started our journey by learning the correct methodology of drawing support and resistance zones!

Trading your first setup

- First of all, identify the current trend of the market by analyzing a longer time frame chart.

- Once you have successfully identified the trend, draw your potential support and resistance zones.

- In general, most currency pairs form a reliable candle stick pattern at significant support and resistance zones. So wait for the candlestick confirmation.

- Last but not least, calculate your potential risk compared to the potential reward. Look for a risk: reward ratio of at least 1:2, or else ignore the trade. Which means, know where your stop loss and profit target will be.

Let's look at some more examples of Price Action trading at Support and Resistance Levels

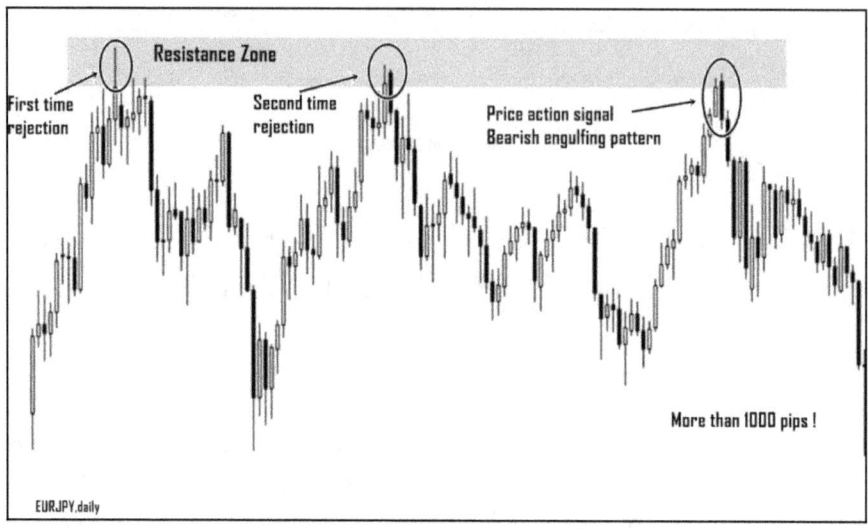

Figure: Bearish engulfing pattern on a strong resistance zone

More than 1000 pips! Don't be surprised, as it's often experienced by a Price Action trader.

Riding 700+ pips in NZD/USD with "Price Action trading strategy"

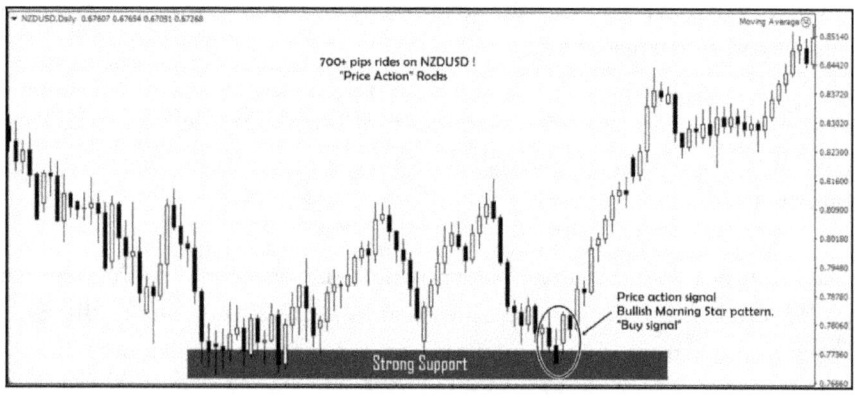

Figure: Bullish Morning Star pattern confirms the big move of 700+pips

You should now be able to identify support and resistance levels. Price Action trading is capable of extremely profitable signals, but don't get carried away and risk all of your capital in a single trade. Traders sometimes incur huge losses by becoming over confident with the Price Action trading results. Some of the rules that professional traders use are as follows:

Rules to follow before you take your trade

- Don't get in the trade too early. Wait for candlestick confirmation.

- Only risk an amount according to your tolerance level.

- Make sure your support and resistance levels or zones are drawn correctly.

- Know where you are going to place your stop loss and have a very good idea of where your target is. This is critical for compliance of your money management rules.

7

HOW TO DRAW PERFECT TREND LINES AND CHANNELS

In this Section, we will learn how to draw a valid trend line and channel. Many Forex Traders incur financial losses in the forex market due to incorrectly marking these on their charts. Before we proceed with this lesson, ensure you have a clear understanding about support and resistance zones.

A trend line is drawn in a way which is very similar to the way support and resistance levels are drawn. The major difference is the angle by which it has been drawn. Support and resistance levels are always horizontal, whereas trend lines are not.

Rules to draw a trend line

- There must be a prevailing trend in the market.

- Connect the most significant swing highs or swing lows.

- Make sure you have at least three points to connect with a single trend line.

Example of a perfectly drawn trend line

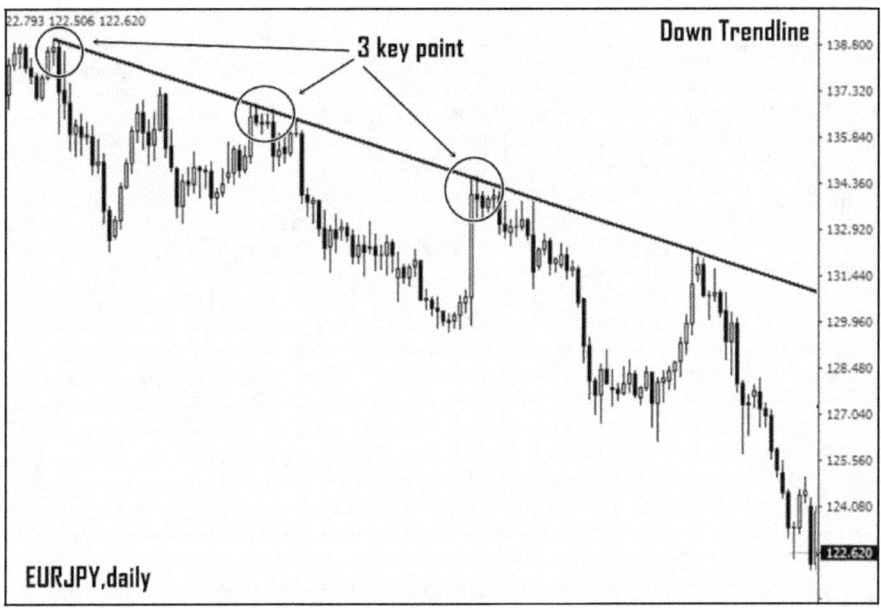

Figure: Perfectly drawn trend line in bearish EUR/JPY

Drawing the channel

Now we will learn how to draw a proper channel. A Channel is also very similar to the trend line and consists of two trend lines which are parallel to each other. You don't need to draw it manually as advanced charting software already has a built-in channel feature.

Rules for drawing a channel

• There should be a prevailing trend in the market. A channel is drawn by two parallel trend lines.

• Two-lines should be perfectly parallel to each other. Consider the slope while drawing a valid channel.

• At least three points should be connected to each other for each individual trend line.

An Example of Channel in EUR/JPY pair

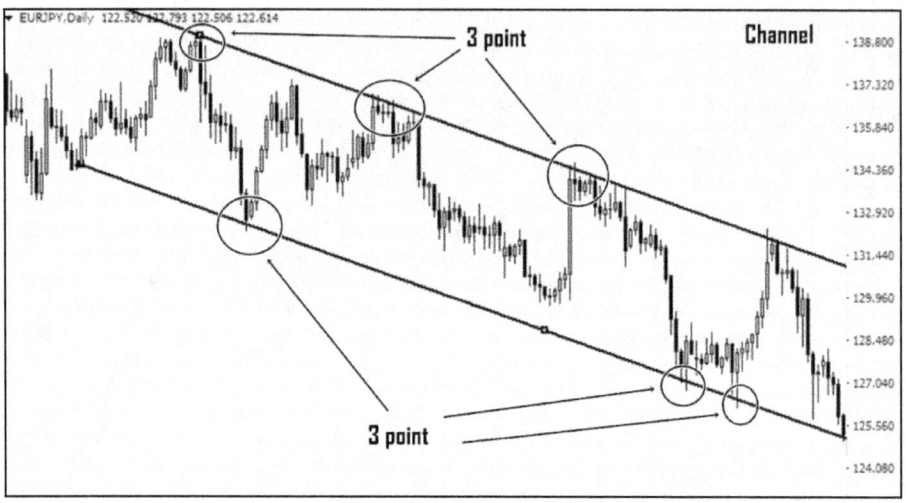

Figure: Perfect 3 point confirmation in upper and lower channel lines

In the case of an uptrend, the formula is simple. Just repeat what you did above, ensuring that the two trend lines that create the channel, both have at least three touching points on the line.

8

PRICE ACTION TRADING SETUP USING TREND LINES AND CHANNELS

Trading the trend lines and channels can be very profitable for Price Action traders as they pick their best trade by using the trend line and channel to their distinct advantage. Price Action trading is nothing but candlestick confirmation in the relevant trading zone. Basically, the trader looks for price action confirmation at the trend line or in the channel.

So why are trend lines and channels so important? The main advantage of trading of the trend line is that you are trading with the trend. It also provides the trader with the unique opportunity to use the smallest possible stop loss.

Take profit and stop loss

Trend line trading and channel trading can be intimidating at times. But if you master the art of drawing perfect trend lines and channels, and have a good understanding of candlestick patterns, then you can be sure that at least the majority of the time, your trades will have a much better chance of being profitable. A trailing stop loss can be used once the trade has started to move in your favor, but initially trend traders usually places a tight stop loss just above or below the candlestick confirmation pattern. At the beginning, you can set your take profit level at a fixed point but this may change as the actual trade progresses, where there may be an opportunity to maximize your profit. If are you are a newbie, then it is best just to set your take profit at the next significant support or resistance level, at least until you become more efficient in reading charts and understanding price movement etc.

Channel trading is very similar to range trading. Whereas range trading represents a market that is basically going sideways, using a Channel normally refers to a market gradually heading in the direction of a distinctive up or down trend, and is usually followed by a strong breakout. A tight stop loss should be used in channel trading and the take profit should be set at the bottom of the channel floor for sell signal. If it's a buy signal then set your take profit would be set at the top channel resistance level.

An example of a sell signal - Trend line trading

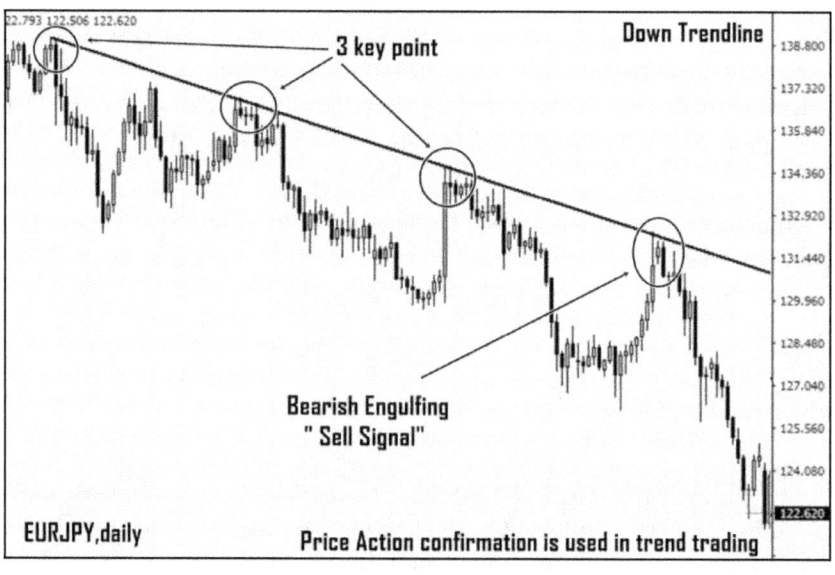

Figure: A perfect sell setup right at the trend line.

Example of a sell signal - Channel Trading

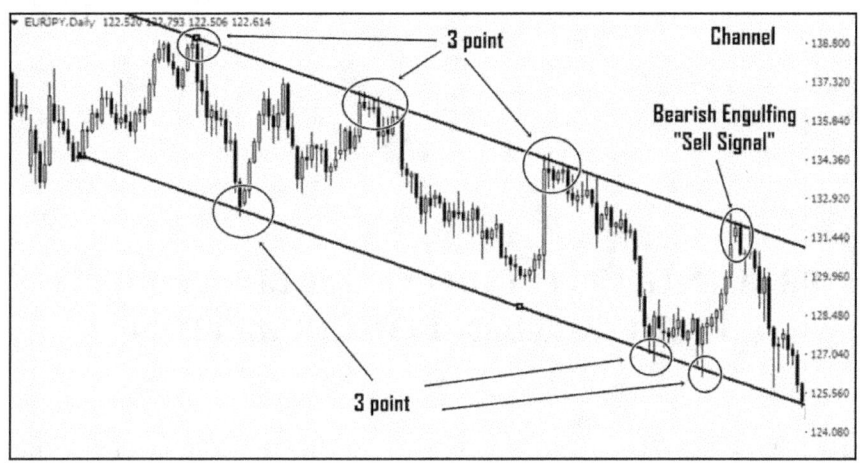

Figure: A perfect sell signal at the channel resistance.

9

TRADING WITH FIBONACCI LEVELS WITH PRICE ACTION CONFIRMATION

The Fibonacci trading strategy is one of the most powerful trading strategies that exists for the long term trader. The trader executes high probability trades on the basis of market retracement and a recent swing high or low.

Why is the Fibonacci trading strategy so popular?

▪ It helps to identify the momentum of a current market trend with high accuracy.

▪ The risk reward ratio in Fibonacci trading system is extremely high.

▪ The trader gets the unique opportunity to trade with the trend.

Fibonacci tools

The Fibonacci tools are a built in function of your trading platform. The trader uses the most recent swing high or swing low to draw their Fibonacci retracement levels. Trading from or to the 61.8%, 50% and 38.2% retracement levels are the most popular among Price Action traders. Confused with this explanation? Well, a simple example will give you a clear insight of a Fibonacci trading example.

Buy signal at a Fibonacci retracement level

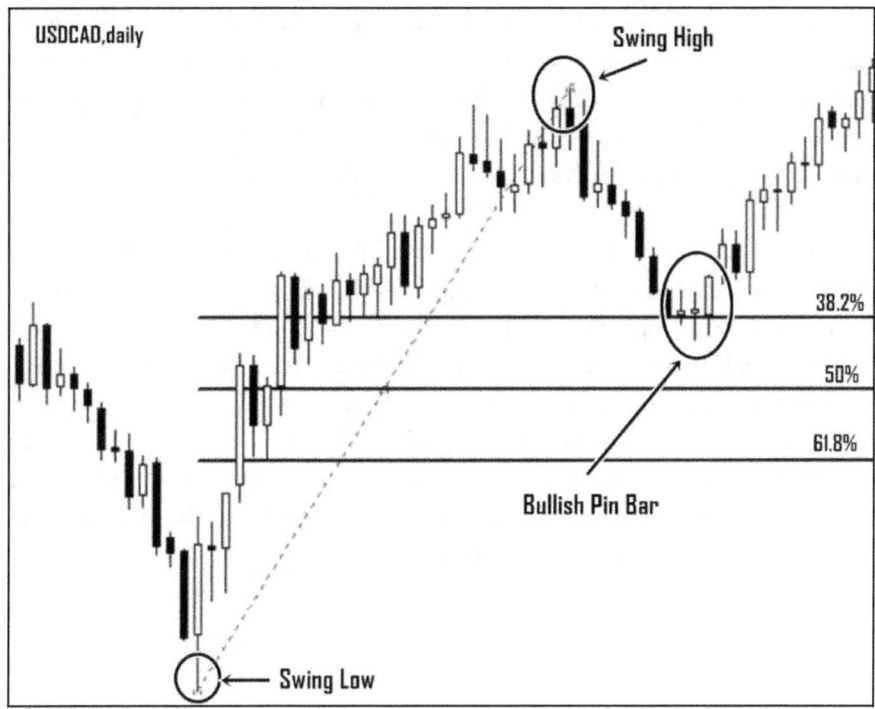

Figure: Price Action confirmation at a Fibonacci Retracement level.

Trade setup

Fibonacci retracement levels work as strong support and resistance levels. Fibonacci levels are drawn from the most recent swing low to swing high for an uptrend. After you have drawn your Fibonacci retracement levels, wait patiently for Price Action confirmation at one of the major retracement areas. As stated previously, the 61.8%, 50% and 38.2% are the most significant retracement levels. In the above trade, a bullish pin bar formed just above the 38.2% retracement area which triggers the buy trade.

Stop loss and take profit

Fibonacci traders should look for a high potential reward before taking the trade. Make sure your risk reward ratio is at least 1:2. Day traders generally put their stop loss just below or above the confirmation candlestick pattern depending on the trade. If you think the stop loss is very tight, then you can put your stop loss just below or above the 61.8 % level.

It is up to you whether you decide to use Fibonacci support and resistance levels as a part of your Price Action trading. It isn't necessary and can sometimes add to signal confusion if the Fibonacci levels don't line up with your original analysis of a trade set up based on other factors such as candlestick pattern confirmation at a trend line. But by using the Fibonacci levels, they can sometimes help confirm a much better trade set up, especially if you also check these levels on a higher time frame. It is a great tool to add to your trading arsenal and you will be pleasantly surprised how accurate these levels are on major trends.

10

IDENTIFYING REVERSAL AND CONTINUATION

This is one of the easiest sections in this book. Many traders strictly follows the proverb, *"the trend is your friend"*, since trading with the trend reduces the margin of error in trading. Surprisingly, many traders struggle to correctly identify the trend in the Forex market.

An uptrend is a trend where the market makes successive higher highs associated with higher lows, whereas in a down trend, the market is making successive lower highs associated with lower lows.

Clear representation of trend formation

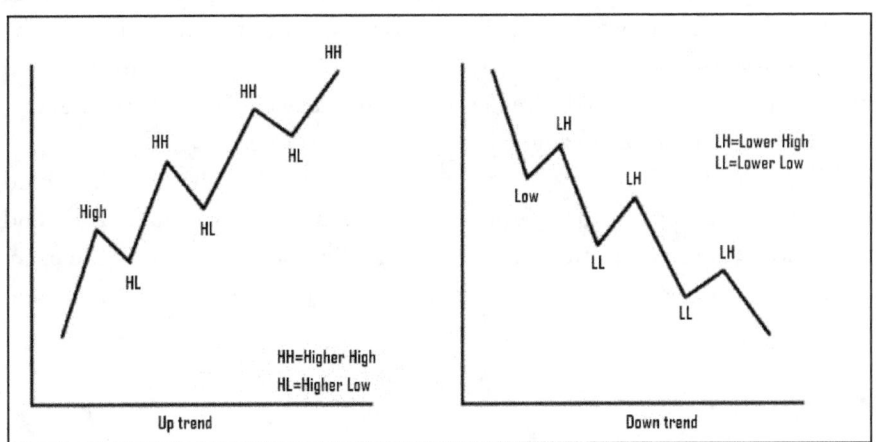

Figure: Trend formation in the Forex market

It sounds pretty easy doesn't it? But remember, many traders fail to identify the trend, or a change in trend, due to not having a proper understanding of trend formation. This simple formula of Highs and Lows will create a firm foundation for trend trading. Swing highs and swing lows are created between support and resistance zones of the forex market. So look for price action confirmation once a swing is complete before entering the trade.

How do we identify a reversal?

Identifying the reversal is very simple in the forex market. Some traders use many complex tools to try and achieve this with minimal success. But to make it simple for you, the moment an uptrend starts to exhibit as a down trend formation pattern, that is the very first indication of a trend reversal. If it's a valid reversal, then sooner or later the market will start creating successive lower highs associated with lower lows, which are the perfect characteristics of a down trend. Remember that all trends eventually reverse, so you want to be aware of this reversal as soon as possible, allowing you to modify your trading plan quickly to take full advantage of any new trades that present.

Identifying trend continuation

Correct identification of a trend continuation is very important for a long term trader. This allows the trader to ride the trade to the end, until the momentum begins to fade. So how can we clearly identify trend continuation? You should already know the answer. If you are thinking about trend formation change then you are absolutely right. A trend will continue in the direction of its momentum until it breaks the trend formation formula. So if an uptrend continues to show higher highs and higher lows, then the uptrend is continuing. Simple as that. It is the exact opposite for a down trend, where it will continue to have lower highs and lower lows.

11

FAKE OUTS AND BREAK OUTS

Trading the fake out and break out can be extremely frustrating in the Forex market. A good understanding of candlestick patterns and a solid trading plan is required to identify each correctly.. The trader must know how to use the correct time period and session to identify the break out and fake out. This sort of trading opportunity typically happens after a major economic news release.

"A Fake out is considered as a false development or false spike in the Forex Market"

As a Price Action trader, you should be able to distinguish between real break outs and fake outs, by confirming both using your knowledge of candlestick patterns. Normally a fake out will not be confirmed, there you would ignore this altogether as it wouldn't qualify as a valid trade. Whereas a genuine break out will normally be confirmed by a candlestick pattern, and here you would take action to enter a possible trade.

Let's see an example of break out and fake out.

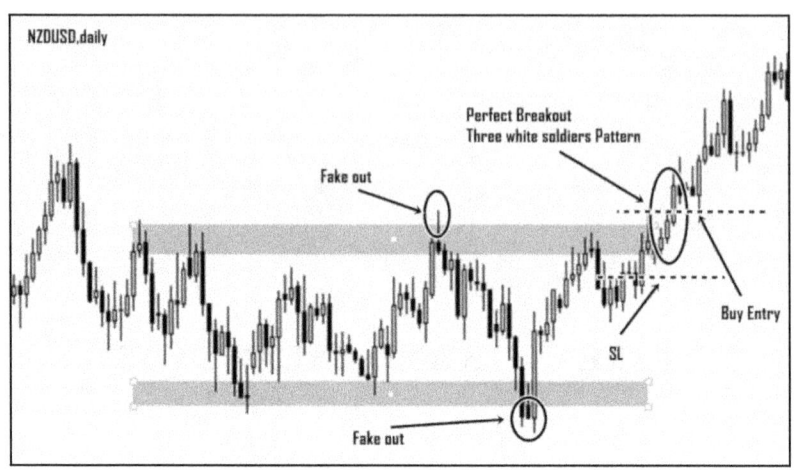

Figure: A break out trade with Price Action confirmation

Trade setup

Like all other trading techniques, break out and fake out trading is also based on support and resistance levels or zones. Price Action traders draw a support and resistance zones for entering into a long or short setup. In the above chart you can clearly see that there were two fake outs. The experienced Price Action trader would ignore the fake outs since they were not confirmed by a legitimate candlestick pattern. Most of the fake outs happen at the time of major economic news releases.

After a specific timeframe followed by a couple of fake outs, the market broke the resistance level with a three white soldier candlestick pattern which is a very bullish signal. A very good opportunity for entering into the long trade, and those who waited patiently were able to trade the breakout successfully with minimal risk as the stop loss was never threatened. Essentially this method depends on patience and immaculate planning. You have to sit tight for the right opportunity. Once the opportunity presents itself, go for the trade, as it has a high probability of being profitable.

Stop loss and take profit

Setting up your stop loss and take profit is very simple in this type of trading strategy. Put your stop loss just above or below the candlestick pattern that confirmed your entry. Some traders set their stop loss below or above the breached support or resistance level. Traders can set their take profit near the next support or resistance level, or consider using a trailing stop behind each minor retracement.

12

RANGE TRADING WITH PRICE ACTION CONFIRMATION

Traders have often seen many pairs operate in a confined region for a long period of time. In Forex terminology this is called a "Ranging Market". Trading the ranging market can be extremely tough unless you have a solid range trading strategy. It is similar to a market within a channel, however a channel normally has a distinct trend either up or down, whereas a ranging market is basically a sideways market with no obvious trend.

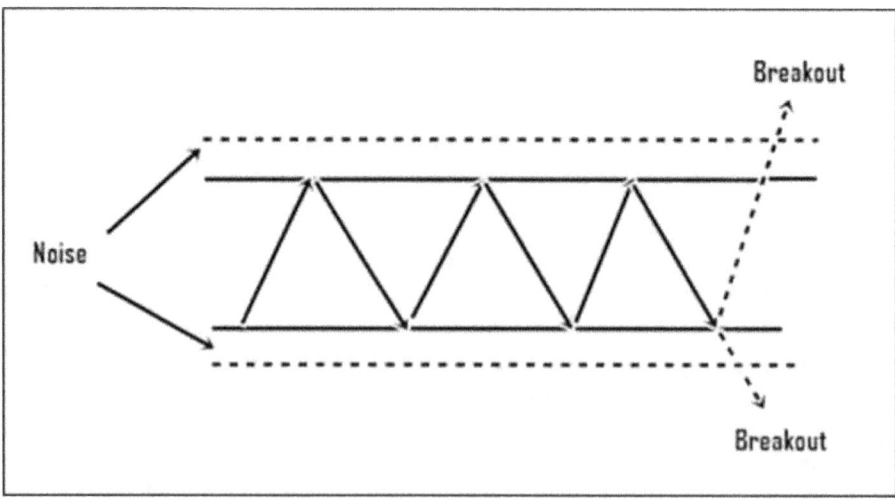

Figure: Ranging market with deadly noise

Trading the ranging market would be a lot simpler if there wasn't a noise zone. So what is Noise? Noise is the false price movement or spike in the currency pair. Price regularly hits the noise zone, triggering your stop loss, and then moves in the direction of your trade without you on it. This can be very frustrating.

Traders should avoid range trading before major economic news releases. These are the fundamental factors that generally cause the market to break out of a range.

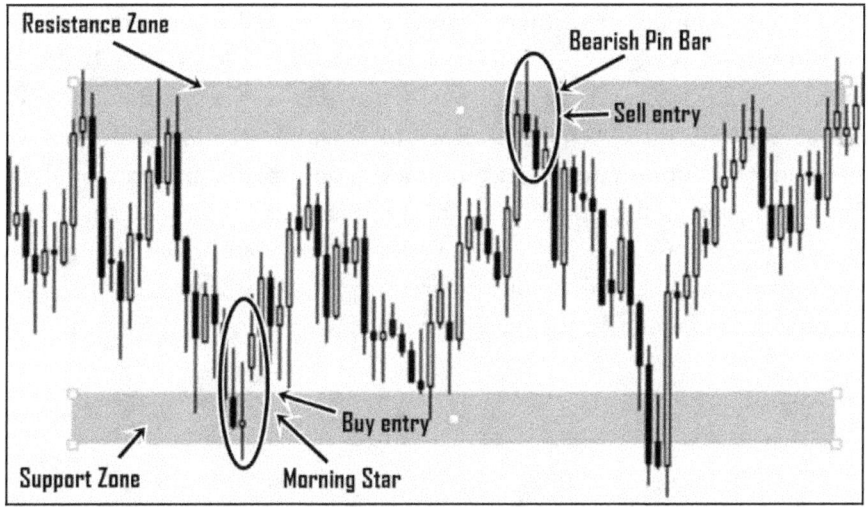

Figure: Range trading with "price action" confirmation

Range trading Setup with Price Action

The ranging market can be extremely profitable if traded with Price Action confirmation. A range trader draws the support and resistance levels before entering into the trade. A trader should wait for the Price Action confirmation before executing their trade. In the above figure, a buy entry was taken by the confirmation of "morning star" pattern on the support zone. Another sell trade was executed since a perfect bearish pin was present at the resistance zone. So basically, you are trading between the support and resistance levels, going from one to the other.

If a valid Price Action setup is confirmed in a support zone or resistance zone, the trader can take their trade. Every Forex trader is familiar with the proverb *"the trend is your friend"*. So if the market goes into a ranging scenario after a recent uptrend, we should consider only taking buy opportunities if you wished to continue trading that pair..

Stop loss and take profit

Traders should use a tight stop loss in range trading. But if there is noise at the relevant support or resistance zone, then the trader should reconsider their stop loss placement. While trading amongst the noise, it's better to have your stop loss well above or below the noise zone. When a buy trade is triggered with Price Action confirmation then the stop loss should be set just below the support zone and candlestick confirmation pattern. Similarly, for a sell signal, the trader should set their stop loss just above the resistance zone or candlestick confirmation pattern. But before taking every single trade, make sure that your risk-reward ratio is at least 1:2, where you are potentially gaining $2 for every $1 risked.

13

PICKING TOPS AND BOTTOMS OF A TRADE WITH PRICE ACTION DURING TREND REVERSALS

Picking tops and bottoms of a pair can be tricky. A seasoned trader always tries to pick the top and bottom of a trade because of its high reward. This type of strategy is only applicable for advanced Price Action traders due to the fact that you are about to take a trade against the trend, which can be a difficult situation for most traders. Price Action traders wait patiently for a candlestick formation at a key support or resistance level in order to execute their trade.

An example of picking top on EUR/JPY pair. Long ride on the down side!

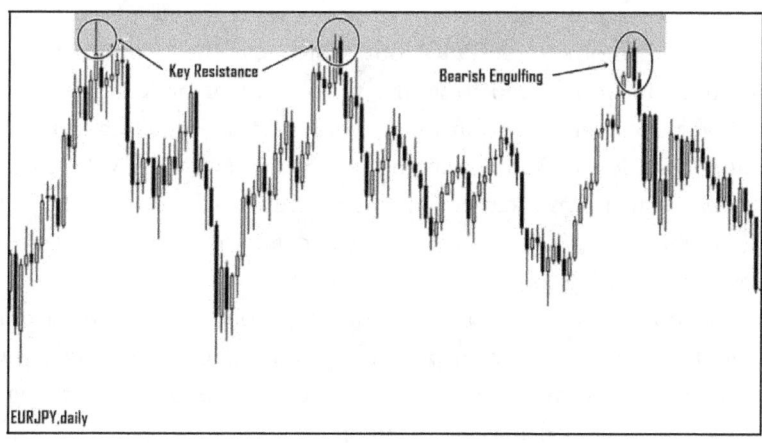

Figure: Riding the trend change by picking the top!

Trade setup

In the above figure, the two key resistance zones have been pointed out at the first and second circles. If the momentum of the trade gradually fades out and fundamental analysis also goes in favor of a trend change, then we will be waiting for a sell signal confirmation at the key resistance level. A bearish engulfing candlestick pattern has been formed in the above chart, which signals that the current bullish trend is ending soon and a new bearish trend is going to be established.

Take Profit and stop loss

Before trading against the trend, extreme precautionary measures should be taken. The stop loss should be very tight, which is just above or below the confirmation candlestick pattern, depending on the trend. Before setting your take profit level make sure you entered the trade by following proper money management rules. Money management are the rules that will help you to manage your losses properly. Having a good risk reward ratio and risking no more than 2% of account equity can be considered as one of the golden rules of money management.

Most Price Action traders use a trailing stop loss when picking the tops and bottoms of a pair. They move their stop loss to break even as soon as the market makes a significant move in the new trend direction and carry their trade until the momentum fades out which can be a pretty long ride! Momentum can be referred to as the movement of price by making new higher highs and higher lows in in uptrend and for down trend, new lower highs and lower lows. All markets move in waves and there will be obvious signs when momentum is either fading or increasing due to the size of these waves, or the steepness of a relevant trend line, or even the size of the retracements, keeping in mind that a market will rarely move in a straight line for a long period. There will always be pullbacks or retracements. Reading charts just comes with practice, practice and more practice, where eventually you get something similar to a sixth sense or a gut feeling, that you just know where price will be heading next.

14

COMMON MISTAKES IN PRICE ACTION TRADING

The Price Action trading strategy is very clear and precise. By correctly following this strategy, every trader should end up an overall profitable trader. *"So why then, is the success rate in Forex Trading so low?"* Because of common mistakes repeated by the trader.

The *"10 most common mistakes"* that Price Action traders make are:

1. Trying to trade against the trend without proper PA confirmation.
2. Risking too much of their account balance due to being overconfident.
3. Considering advice from too many other trading gurus.
4. Choosing the wrong time frame while identifying the trade and trend reversal.
5. Setting the stop loss too close to the confirming candlestick pattern.
6. Forcing trend lines and channels to join the minimum three points for validation.
7. Ignoring the major economic news releases and trend changes.
8. Trading without proper money management rules.
9. Faulty candlestick pattern identification.
10. Considering the support and resistance levels as a fixed line rather than a zone.

As a professional trader, it is important that you keep a Trading Journal of all your individual trades, whether they be winning or losing trades. With this information, you can go back and research where you went wrong and where you went right. Here you can possibly identify a common mistake that you may be making, so you can avoid it in future trades. This journal will also help with future trade management due to the fact that you are collating more and more results as your trading continues, and hopefully improving. I can't stress enough how important it is to keep some sort of detailed record of your trading.

15

LAST WORDS

Well, congratulations! You have made it to the end and should have a good understanding of what Price Action trading is all about. As you can see, it is a relatively simple method of trading without cluttering up your charts with multiple indicators. It provides very clear set ups of high probability trades, if you follow the information provided in this book. Like any trading method, you will have losing trades. That is just a part of the game. But with Price Action trading, you should win way more than you lose, and also your risk to reward ratio is very high which overall, lends itself to a high win percentage as well as a high profitability rate, with little stress involved.

This style of trading may not suit everyone, as it does take some practice in getting use to drawing good trend lines or channels, and also recognizing candlestick patterns. What I would suggest you do, is bring up some charts and go back through the chart history one candle at a time looking for set ups. You can practice drawing on the charts and identifying the support and resistance levels etc. Stick with the higher time frames as they tend to give cleaner trends without all the daily noise of the markets. Also it may pay to print out a template of your preferred candlestick patterns, so you can refer to it as you do your research. You will eventually recognize these patterns at a glance as they will become quite clear to you after some serious chart study.

You would have noticed generally the same theme throughout this book. All that is required is that you trade off or through some resistance or support level, whether that be a trend line, channel or a range etc, and using candlestick patterns to confirm the potential market move. It is that simple. No need to complicate things. If you are wrong, take the small loss due to your excellent money management rules, and then get ready for the next trade.

My final advice to you is about Money Management. At the end of the day, we all want to make money from trading. That is the end goal. To make money, you need money in your account, so capital preservation is very important. Start trading small until you get use to the method and you can collate some results to give you a 'big picture' on how you are going. Once you are comfortable, then you can slowly increase your position size. But don't bet the farm on one trade. Be sensible about it and keep it in the 1-3% risk per trade. There will be losers, so don't get too concerned about them, just learn from them, and then forget about them. Concentrate on the next new trade presenting and don't make the same mistakes.

All the best,

Michelle

Free downloadable MT4 Forex Trading Robot (EA, Expert Advisor)

Would you be interested in receiving the Trading Robot associated with my other book? *Forex: A Powerful MT4 Trading Robot to Maximize Profits:*

The International Amazon Link is provided below if you would like further details (case sensitive):

http://lrd.to/Forex-Trading-Robot

To find out how you can download the SMSF Trading Robot, designed for the MT4 platform, simply go to the following link (*case sensitive*) and you will be provided with finer details:

http://eepurl.com/b7XjD1

A reminder. I have pulled together a few helpful Printouts from the book for you which you can access from the following link:

The printouts include:

- How to read a candlestick
- 15 of the most important candlesticks
- The Top 5 most reliable candlestick patterns
- Support and Resistance Levels
- Clear representation of trend formation

The printouts can be accessed here:
http://bit.ly/price-action-download
*The above is 'case sensitive'.

Please remember, if you use AOL, Yahoo, Gmail or Hotmail, these providers deliver mail in small batches which can sometimes result in emails taking up to 24 hours to come through.

*Please check your spam/junk folders, if nothing comes through. Failing all the above, if it doesn't arrive, drop me a line at: MM.ForexRobots@gmail.com

ABOUT THE AUTHOR

Michelle Michaels has had an interest in trading the financial markets dating back to the late 90's, when she first tried her hand at Futures trading. This was followed by Stock and Options trading and she eventually settled on concentrating all of her efforts into Forex trading in 2004. This has been her passion since, and she has had some great success along the way.

Michelle eventually realized that her trading style could be used across all financial markets. Primarily a Swing Trader, trading from the 4hr and Daily charts, Michelle also has a strong interest in different trading methods and converting those methods into trading robots (algorithmic trading) on the popular Metatrader (MT4) platform. As Michelle is now settled on her trading methods and enjoying the profits from it, in her quiet time she shares her knowledge with other traders and those new to the trading world regarding what she has learned along the way.